Welcome to Good Morning Girls! We are so glad you are joining us.

God created us to walk with Him, to know Him, and to be loved by Him. He is our living well, and when we drink from the water He continually provides, His living water will change the entire course of our lives.

> *Jesus said: "Whoever drinks of the water that I will give him will never be thirsty again. The water that I will give him will become in him a spring of water welling up to eternal life." ~ John 4:14 (ESV)*

So let's begin.

The method we use here at GMG is called the **SOAK** method.

- ❑ **S**—The S stands for *Scripture*—Read the chapter for the day. Then choose 1-2 verses and write them out word for word. (There is no right or wrong choice—just let the Holy Spirit guide you.)

- ❑ **O**—The O stands for *Observation*—Look at the verse or verses you wrote out. Write 1 or 2 observations. What stands out to you? What do you learn about the character of God from these verses? Is there a promise, command or teaching?

- ❑ **A**—The A stands for *Application*—Personalize the verses. What is God saying to you? How can you apply them to your life? Are there any changes you need to make or an action to take?

- ❑ **K**—The K stands for *Kneeling in Prayer*—Pause, kneel and pray. Confess any sin God has revealed to you today. Praise God for His word. Pray the passage over your own life or someone you love. Ask God to help you live out your applications.

SOAK God's word into your heart and squeeze every bit of nourishment you can out of each day's scripture reading. Soon you will find your life transformed by the renewing of your mind!

Walk with the King!

Courtney

WomenLivingWell.org, GoodMorningGirls.org

Join the GMG Community

WomenLivingWell.org | GoodMorningGirls.org

Facebook.com/WomenLivingwell | Facebook.com/GoodMorningGirlsWLW

Instagram.com/WomenLivingWell #WomenLivingWell

#MakingYourHomeAHaven

Slowing Down
for
SPIRITUAL GROWTH

MAKING YOUR
HOME
a haven

A 4-WEEK BIBLE STUDY
by Courtney Joseph

GMG Bible Coloring Chart

COLORS	KEYWORDS
PURPLE	God, Jesus, Holy Spirit, Saviour, Messiah
PINK	women of the Bible, family, marriage, parenting, friendship, relationships
RED	love, kindness, mercy, compassion, peace, grace
GREEN	faith, obedience, growth, fruit, salvation, fellowship, repentance
YELLOW	worship, prayer, praise, doctrine, angels, miracles, power of God, blessings
BLUE	wisdom, teaching, instruction, commands
ORANGE	prophecy, history, times, places, kings, genealogies, people, numbers, covenants, vows, visions, oaths, future
BROWN/GRAY	Satan, sin, death, hell, evil, idols, false teachers, hypocrisy, temptation

TABLE OF CONTENTS

Introduction

Welcome to the *Making Your Home a Haven* Bible Study! Twelve years ago, I began this series online at WomenLivingWell.org. Never could I have imagined how much it would resonate with so many women around the world. I pray this study blesses you in the same way!

If you have been feeling disconnected from God or if you have a desire to go deeper in your walk with the Lord, then this study is for you.

God's pace is much slower than this world's pace.

We must slow down to catch up with God.

We must create calm moments in our day because it's in the unhurried moments that we can clearly see and hear the voice of God.

This Bible Study is going to help you slow down. It is going to force you to pause every day and enter into the presence of our Almighty God through thanksgiving, prayer and the reading of God's Word.

Self-care is a very popular concept these days, but I believe that soul care IS self-care. So, let's take care of our souls by intentionally creating a physical environment in our homes, as well as a spiritual environment, that brings us closer to God. As a result, we will experience peace and a sense of calmness inside our souls, no matter what we are facing.

Each week, I will provide for you a practical challenge of something I do in my home that makes it more of a haven. I hope you will take the challenges. They do make a difference!

Each weekday, we will pause, give thanks, pray and meditate on God's Word through SOAKing in the daily scripture reading for the day.

Also, online at WomenLivingWell.org, you will find four videos—one per week—that correspond with the scriptures we are studying.

I encourage you to give yourself permission to not have your to-do list all checked off in order for you to slow down and catch up with God.

David writes in Psalm 42:1, 2:

> "As the deer pants for streams of water,
>   so my soul pants for you, my God.
> ² My soul thirsts for God, for the living God.
>   When can I go and meet with God?"

I pray that your time spent in God's Word will bless your soul and quench your thirst and that you will live well, as you drink from the living well, the living words of God. (John 4:13-14)

I can't wait to take this journey with you!

Keep Walking with the King,

Courtney

Week 1: Slowing Down with Silence and Solitude

For God alone my soul waits in silence.

Psalm 62:1

Silence and solitude open the door to communion with God.

If we want to grow spiritually, we have to love a life of prayer and reading God's word. We have to go in deeper with God and commune with him. We have to practice the presence of God and not just give him a laundry list of prayer requests but listen – really listen to him as well.

Behind the noise of life – there is silence. Silence is the background to life. But once we are silent, we are not actually silent because that is when we hear our self-talk and our inner thoughts. Sometimes being alone with our thoughts can be scary. Dark thoughts of anger, bitterness, or pain might bubble up under the surface, but this is where spiritual growth and even spiritual warfare takes place.

Some call our time alone in silence and solitude with the Lord a "quiet time". Others call this time their "devotional" time. Essentially, it is a time devoted to being quiet with the Lord and communing with him.

Jesus' Example:

- Jesus inaugurated His ministry by spending forty days alone in the desert. (Matthew 4:1-11)
- Before Jesus chose the twelve disciples, He spent the entire night alone. (Luke 6:12)
- When the disciples had finished a long day with the crowds, Jesus instructed them, "Come away by yourselves to a desolate place and rest a while." (Mark 6:31)
- Following the healing of the leper, Jesus withdrew alone to the wilderness to pray. (Luke 5:16)

If Jesus needed silence and solitude to commune with God, then certainly we do too!

Now, let's get practical and make a plan.

1. **Plan Where: Plan your solitary place.**
   I encourage you to create a place that is inviting and that is ready and waiting

for you, free of distractions. This may be at your kitchen table, your favorite recliner, a place outdoors, in your car or even a coffee shop.

2. **Plan How: Plan how you will spend your quiet time.**
   All you really need is your Bible but you may want to create a basket or bag of quiet time goodies that includes a journal, notecards, pens, highlighters, or colored pencils. Maybe you'll want to follow a Bible Reading Plan, purchase a Bible Study book, do your own word study, read a Proverb or Psalm a day or work on Bible memorization.

3. **Plan When: Plan what time you will meet with God daily.**
   The best way to stay disciplined with your daily quiet time is to plan a time to meet with God and try to stick to each day, as best as you can. Once you begin to repeat your plan over and over, soon you will birth a habit and it will be much easier to practice silence and solitude with the Lord.

The reality is we live in a busy and noisy culture where it is hard to simply sit still at the feet of Jesus. Have you felt it? Have you felt the battle for your attention?

1 Peter 5:8 says the enemy is a roaring lion, seeking whom he may devour. The roar of a lion is loud! The enemy is loud, and he wants to distract us. We must fight against distraction and busyness and one way we can battle effectively is by having a plan that creates the habit and discipline for intimacy with God and spiritual growth.

God loves you so much! He died on the cross, so we could be forgiven of all of our sins. He wants to meet with us and hear from us and speak to us, but we must slow down so we can listen.

So, it's time! It's time to take 15 minutes a day to get alone and be silent and be grateful, pray, meditate and commune with the Lord and then go forward with the day, delighting in the good gifts God has given us to enjoy. Let's get started..

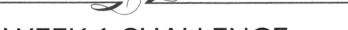

WEEK 1 CHALLENGE

Go buy an extra-large candle and light your candle every day in your home. Each time the glimmer of the candle catches your eye, stop, pray and give thanks.

I will be starting my candle in the morning, but you can start yours at dinnertime or whenever is convenient for you. I will be placing mine in the kitchen—the main hub of my home.

{Share your pictures of your candle on Instagram by using the hashtags: #MakingYourHomeAHaven and #WomenLivingWell}

DAY 1

The Lord is my shepherd: I shall not want.
He makes me lie down in green pastures.
He leads me beside still waters.

Psalm 23:1-2

Things I Am Grateful for Today:

_____

_____

_____

_____

_____

_____

_____

Things I Am Praying for Today:

_____

_____

_____

_____

_____

_____

_____

Psalm 23:1~2

S—The S stands for *Scripture*

O—The O stands for *Observation*

A—The A stands for *Application*

K—The K stands for *Kneeling in Prayer*

DAY 2

He restores my soul.
He leads me in paths of righteousness for his name's sake.
Psalm 23:3

Things I Am Grateful for Today:

_____

_____

_____

_____

_____

_____

_____

_____

Things I Am Praying for Today:

_____

_____

_____

_____

_____

_____

_____

_____

Psalm 23:3

S—The S stands for ***Scripture***

O—The O stands for ***Observation***

A—The A stands for ***Application***

K—The K stands for ***Kneeling in Prayer***

DAY 3

*Even though I walk through the valley of the shadow of death,
I will fear no evil, for you are with me;
your rod and your staff, they comfort me.*

Psalm 23:4

Things I Am Grateful for Today:

_____

_____

_____

_____

_____

_____

_____

Things I Am Praying for Today:

_____

_____

_____

_____

_____

_____

_____

_____

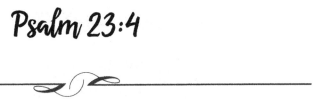

Psalm 23:4

S—The S stands for *Scripture*

O—The O stands for *Observation*

A—The A stands for *Application*

K—The K stands for *Kneeling in Prayer*

DAY 4

You prepare a table before me
in the presence of my enemies:
you anoint my head with oil; my cup overflows.

Psalm 23:5

Things I Am Grateful for Today:

_____

_____

_____

_____

_____

_____

_____

Things I Am Praying for Today:

_____

_____

_____

_____

_____

_____

_____

_____

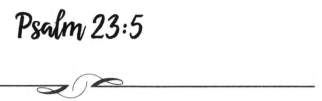

Psalm 23:5

S—The S stands for **Scripture**

O—The O stands for **Observation**

A—The A stands for **Application**

K—The K stands for **Kneeling in Prayer**

DAY 5

Surely goodness and mercy shall follow me all the days of my life,
and I shall dwell in the house of the Lord forever.

Psalm 23:6

Things I Am Grateful for Today:

_____

_____

_____

_____

_____

_____

_____

Things I Am Praying for Today:

_____

_____

_____

_____

_____

_____

_____

_____

_____

Psalm 23:6

S—The S stands for **Scripture**

O—The O stands for **Observation**

A—The A stands for **Application**

K—The K stands for **Kneeling in Prayer**

Week 2: Slowing Down to Study God's Word

His delight is in the law of the Lord,
and on his law he meditates day and night.

Psalm 1:2

There is no short cut for spiritual growth.

Connecting with God on a deeper level requires time. We must slow down and get away from the distractions of this world to read the Bible. Our souls need to drink deeply from God's living well.

The world's rhythm is work, work, work. God's rhythm is work, rest, work, rest, work, rest. In order to rest, we have to trust in the Lord that he will take care of everything, even when we are resting. Some of us only rest when we are sick, but we are burning ourselves out. We were all built with limits and God is inviting us to stop the rhythm of the world, slow down and go deeper with him.

Now, studying God's word can be as simple or complex as you'd like it to be. Here's some ideas of ways you can study God's Word:

- Open to page one and begin reading in Genesis and read a few chapters a day until you get to the end in Revelation.
- Do word studies and look up the original Greek and Hebrew words and their meanings.
- Do a word study on something you are struggling with, like anger, worry, fear, joy or forgiving others.
- Study a theological area like grace, faith, sanctification, or the return of Jesus.
- Look into family matters in the Bible like what God says about children, marriage, or friendships.
- Use the SOAK method to study through a book of the Bible – one chapter a day.
- Go online to BibleGateway.com and research key

It is in our hidden life of meeting with God in Bible study and prayer that we are strengthened to face the trials and spiritual battles ahead. No one knows what is around the next corner but the time we have spent in his word prepares us for whatever lies ahead.

Do not mistake the unseen hidden rhythms of slowing down and meeting with the Lord as unimportant. They are vital to your spiritual core strength and spiritual growth. God is present with you. Practice the presence of God by simply slowing down and being with him in his word. He loves you so much.

WEEK 2 CHALLENGE

Keep your candle going and add to it—soft music every day in your home. Choose worship, classical or another form of peaceful music that helps you focus on the Lord.

My candle and soft music literally change the atmosphere of my home. While the rest of my home may be messy, my candle keeps on burning and my soft music keeps on playing. Morning, noon and night they serve me. My candle serves me with a flickering warm light, a pleasant scent, and a reminder to turn to God as my source of strength and help. My music serves me with a soothing sound. They don't make messes, they don't need managed, they just simply bless me and my family. I hope it blesses you too.

{Share your pictures of your favorite Worship CD or playlist on Instagram by using the hashtags: #MakingYourHomeAHaven and #WomenLivingWell}

DAY 1

Blessed is the man who walks not in the counsel of the wicked,
nor stands in the way of sinners, nor sits in the seat of scoffers.
Psalm 1:1

Things I Am Grateful for Today:

_____

_____

_____

_____

_____

_____

_____

Things I Am Praying for Today:

_____

_____

_____

_____

_____

_____

_____

Psalm 1:1

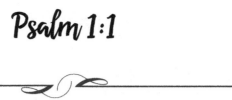

S—The S stands for *Scripture*

O—The O stands for *Observation*

A—The A stands for *Application*

K—The K stands for *Kneeling in Prayer*

DAY 2

But his delight is in the law of the Lord,
and on his law he meditates day and night.

Psalm 1:2

Things I Am Grateful for Today:

_____

_____

_____

_____

_____

_____

_____

_____

Things I Am Praying for Today:

_____

_____

_____

_____

_____

_____

_____

_____

_____

Psalm 1:2

S—The S stands for **Scripture**

O—The O stands for **Observation**

A—The A stands for **Application**

K—The K stands for **Kneeling in Prayer**

DAY 3

He is like a tree planted by streams of water
that yields its fruit in its season, and its leaf does not wither.
In all that he does, he prospers.

Psalm 1:3

Things I Am Grateful for Today:

_____

_____

_____

_____

_____

_____

_____

Things I Am Praying for Today:

_____

_____

_____

_____

_____

_____

_____

Psalm 1:3

S—The S stands for *Scripture*

O—The O stands for *Observation*

A—The A stands for *Application*

K—The K stands for *Kneeling in Prayer*

DAY 4

The wicked are not so, but are like chaff that the wind drives away.
Therefore the wicked will not stand in the judgment,
nor sinners in the congregation of the righteous.

Psalm 1:4~5

Things I Am Grateful for Today:

_____

_____

_____

_____

_____

_____

_____

Things I Am Praying for Today:

_____

_____

_____

_____

_____

_____

_____

_____

Psalm 1:4-5

S—The S stands for **Scripture**

O—The O stands for **Observation**

A—The A stands for **Application**

K—The K stands for **Kneeling in Prayer**

DAY 5

For the Lord knows the way of the righteous,
but the way of the wicked will perish.

Psalm 1:6

Things I Am Grateful for Today:

_____

_____

_____

_____

_____

_____

_____

Things I Am Praying for Today:

_____

_____

_____

_____

_____

_____

_____

_____

Psalm 1:6

S—The S stands for *Scripture*

O—The O stands for *Observation*

A—The A stands for *Application*

K—The K stands for *Kneeling in Prayer*

Week 3: Slowing Down for Supplication and Prayer

I waited patiently for the Lord;
he inclined to me and heard my cry.

Psalm 40:1

God is already right there with you – you only need to acknowledge his presence.

When we slow down to pray, we grow spiritually and as we grow, our intimacy with God goes deeper. But when God's response is slow, we can grow impatient. We are used to the click of a mouse. We click and the response is quick. Over and over, we can repeat the quick response. But with God, sometimes we pray and then we have to wait...and wait...and wait. It can be tempting to replace prayer with positive thinking, formulas and mouse clicking. But as children of the Lord, we must do it differently.

It takes effort to walk with the Lord daily because...let's be real for a second, sometimes praying the same thing day in and day out can get boring. If you are praying the same things over and over – like praying for your family, friends, finances, the church, and people's crisis – it can get repetitive.

So, switch it up friends! Pray the Bible. Take one verse from Psalms or one verse from Proverbs and pray it over your family and your friends.

For example, take Psalm 40 verse 1. It says "I waited patiently for the Lord." Pray this over your children. "Lord, please help my children to wait patiently for you." Pray this over your friends. "Lord, please strengthen my friends in their waiting."

Then move on to the next line. Pray God's word line by line over your loved ones and if a verse does not apply, skip it. You can do this using some of the New Testament letters as well.

We were made to be connected to God. Our soul needs to be anchored to Christ. God wants us to have peace and he tells us the way to get there is by turning our worries over to him, by prayer and supplication.

What is prayer? Prayer is simply talking to God.

What is supplication? It is humbly making a request of God and usually it is something we strongly desire.

So, this week, let's practice the presence of God every single day through focused prayer and supplication. Let's bring our outer world and inner world into harmony through prayer. God loves you and is with you and he wants to hear from you.

WEEK 3 CHALLENGE

Go pick a bouquet of flowers from your garden or a nearby field or buy yourself a small bouquet. Each time you see the flowers, be reminded of God's love and presence with you. Our creator God is listening to your prayers.

I will be purchasing a small bouquet from my grocery store and placing it in a vase, in my kitchen.

{Share your pictures of your flowers on Instagram by using the hashtags: #MakingYourHomeAHaven and #WomenLivingWell}

DAY 1

*I waited patiently for the Lord;
he inclined to me and heard my cry.*

Psalm 40:1

Things I Am Grateful for Today:

_____

_____

_____

_____

_____

_____

_____

Things I Am Praying for Today:

_____

_____

_____

_____

_____

_____

_____

_____

Psalm 40:1

S—The S stands for **Scripture**

O—The O stands for **Observation**

A—The A stands for **Application**

K—The K stands for **Kneeling in Prayer**

DAY 2

He drew me up from the pit of destruction, out of the miry bog,
and set my feet upon a rock, making my steps secure.

Psalm 40:2

Things I Am Grateful for Today:

_____

_____

_____

_____

_____

_____

_____

Things I Am Praying for Today:

_____

_____

_____

_____

_____

_____

_____

_____

Psalm 40:2

S—The S stands for *Scripture*

O—The O stands for *Observation*

A—The A stands for *Application*

K—The K stands for *Kneeling in Prayer*

DAY 3

He put a new song in my mouth, a song of praise to our God.
Many will see and fear, and put their trust in the Lord.

Psalm 40:3

Things I Am Grateful for Today:

_____

_____

_____

_____

_____

_____

_____

Things I Am Praying for Today:

_____

_____

_____

_____

_____

_____

_____

_____

_____

Psalm 40:3

S—The S stands for **Scripture**

O—The O stands for **Observation**

A—The A stands for **Application**

K—The K stands for **Kneeling in Prayer**

DAY 4

Blessed is the man who makes the Lord his trust,
who does not turn to the proud, to those who go astray after a lie!

Psalm 40:4

Things I Am Grateful for Today:

_____

_____

_____

_____

_____

_____

_____

_____

Things I Am Praying for Today:

_____

_____

_____

_____

_____

_____

_____

_____

Psalm 40:4

S—The S stands for *Scripture*

O—The O stands for *Observation*

A—The A stands for *Application*

K—The K stands for *Kneeling in Prayer*

DAY 5

You have multiplied, O Lord my God, your wondrous deeds and your thoughts toward us; none can compare with you!
I will proclaim and tell of them, yet they are more than can be told.
Psalm 40:5

Things I Am Grateful for Today:

_____

_____

_____

_____

_____

_____

_____

Things I Am Praying for Today:

_____

_____

_____

_____

_____

_____

_____

_____

_____

Psalm 40:5

S—The S stands for ***Scripture***

O—The O stands for ***Observation***

A—The A stands for ***Application***

K—The K stands for ***Kneeling in Prayer***

Week 4: Slowing Down to Celebrate

Oh come, let us sing to the Lord;
let us make a joyful noise to the rock of our salvation!

Psalm 95:1

David tells us to make a joyful noise to the Lord.

When was the last time you made a joyful noise to the Lord? Was it an hour ago, a day ago, a week ago or when?

It is good for our souls to slow down and celebrate our salvation.

It is good for our souls to slow down and celebrate God's faithfulness.

Does life sometimes feel like a blur? One day bleeds into the next and the next and before you know it, another month and then year has passed?

God wants us to savor the moments and find joy in the present and the only way we can do that is by slowing down. Once we slow down and assess our lives, we can see that there are many things to both celebrate and give thanks to God for.

When we are busy and on the go, we fail to celebrate all the good things in our lives. And while we have special holidays for celebrating like Thanksgiving, Christmas and Easter, we need to remember that each day we can celebrate God's goodness to us.

I'm reminded of the early church and how they were persecuted and suffering and yet Paul told them to "rejoice always". How could they possibly do that? They couldn't in their own strength, but joy is a fruit of the Spirit. Joy comes from God. In God's strength, we can always have joy and a song in our heart, even in the worst times.

Edith Shaeffer says:

"We are an environment, each one of us.

We are an environment for the other people with whom we live, the people with whom we work, the people with whom we communicate...our conversations, attitudes, behavior, response or lack of response, hardness or compassion, our love or selfishness, joy or dullness, concern for others or self pity – all these things make a difference to the people who have to live in our environment."

Have you ever considered that YOU are an environment? What type of environment are you?

- Are you the warm and hospitable type?
- Are you the cheery, sunshine type?
- Are you calm and quiet?
- Harried and hurried?
- Irritable and angry?
- Or perhaps tired and ticked-off?
- What type of environment are you?

Life is certainly not all butterflies and roses…but because we are Christians – we are to reflect Christ in our environment.

So, let's take time this week in our homes to celebrate the little things. Perhaps celebrating a day's hard work looks like hot cocoa with marshmallows and a good book or maybe it's a bubble bath with soft music going, or maybe it's throwing a bonfire and inviting your friends and family to make s'mores. For others, maybe it's cranking up the music in your kitchen and having a dance party or maybe it's taking a friend out for dinner to celebrate the gift of your friendship. Whatever is good in your life – celebrate it!

Make a joyful noise to the Lord.

God is so good! He is worthy!

Keep walking with the King!

WEEK 4 CHALLENGE

Seek out a place of solitude to get alone with God. Stop your work, turn off your phone, the television, music and computer. Be still. Go outside or find a place in your home, where you can be alone and simply rest and be at peace. Practice the presence of God.

Rest is a need—not a want. Rest is not optional or something we wait to do when we are retired. Rest is a blessing from the Lord, and it requires humility to admit we need it. I'll be running a bubble bath and probably taking a much-needed nap this week. Soul care is self-care. So, enjoy it!

{Share your pictures of your favorite place to rest on Instagram by using the hashtags: #MakingYourHomeAHaven and #WomenLivingWell}

DAY 1

Oh come, let us sing to the Lord;
let us make a joyful noise to the rock of our salvation!

Psalm 95:1

Things I Am Grateful for Today:

_____

_____

_____

_____

_____

_____

_____

Things I Am Praying for Today:

_____

_____

_____

_____

_____

_____

_____

_____

_____

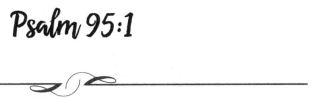

Psalm 95:1

S—The S stands for *Scripture*

O—The O stands for *Observation*

A—The A stands for *Application*

K—The K stands for *Kneeling in Prayer*

DAY 2

Let us come into his presence with thanksgiving:
let us make a joyful noise to him with songs of praise!

Psalm 95:2

Things I Am Grateful for Today:

_____

_____

_____

_____

_____

_____

_____

Things I Am Praying for Today:

_____

_____

_____

_____

_____

_____

_____

_____

S—The S stands for **Scripture**

O—The O stands for **Observation**

A—The A stands for **Application**

K—The K stands for **Kneeling in Prayer**

DAY 3

For the Lord is a great God,
and a great King above all gods.

Psalm 95:3

Things I Am Grateful for Today:

_____

_____

_____

_____

_____

_____

_____

Things I Am Praying for Today:

_____

_____

_____

_____

_____

_____

_____

Psalm 95:3

S—The S stands for **Scripture**

O—The O stands for **Observation**

A—The A stands for **Application**

K—The K stands for **Kneeling in Prayer**

DAY 4

In his hand are the depths of the earth; the heights of the mountains are his also.

Psalm 95:4

Things I Am Grateful for Today:

_____

_____

_____

_____

_____

_____

_____

_____

Things I Am Praying for Today:

_____

_____

_____

_____

_____

_____

_____

_____

Psalm 95:4

S—The S stands for **Scripture**

O—The O stands for **Observation**

A—The A stands for **Application**

K—The K stands for **Kneeling in Prayer**

DAY 5

The sea is his, for he made it, and his hands formed the dry land.
Oh come, let us worship and bow down: let us kneel before the Lord, our Maker!

Psalm 95:5~6

Things I Am Grateful for Today:

_____

_____

_____

_____

_____

_____

_____

Things I Am Praying for Today:

_____

_____

_____

_____

_____

_____

_____

_____

Psalm 95:5~6

S—The S stands for **Scripture**

O—The O stands for **Observation**

A—The A stands for **Application**

K—The K stands for **Kneeling in Prayer**

Video Notes

(go to WomenLivingWell.org to find the weekly corresponding videos)

Made in the USA
Las Vegas, NV
27 October 2021